To:

The Love of my life. Be good. Love

Sandy

Love
Isn't Always
Easy

Other books by

Blue Mountain Press INC.

Come Into the Mountains, Dear Friend
by Susan Polis Schutz
I Want to Laugh, I Want to Cry
by Susan Polis Schutz
Peace Flows from the Sky
by Susan Polis Schutz
Someone Else to Love
by Susan Polis Schutz
I'm Not That Kind of Girl
by Susan Polis Schutz
Yours If You Ask
by Susan Polis Schutz
Love, Live and Share
by Susan Polis Schutz
Find Happiness In Everything You Do
by Susan Polis Schutz

The Language of Friendship
The Language of Love
The Language of Happiness
The Desiderata of Happiness
by Max Ehrmann
I Care About Your Happiness
by Kahlil Gibran/Mary Haskell
I Wish You Good Spaces
Gordon Lightfoot
We Are All Children Searching for Love
by Leonard Nimoy
Come Be with Me
by Leonard Nimoy
Creeds to Love and Live By
On the Wings of Friendship
You've Got a Friend
Carole King
With You There and Me Here
The Dawn of Friendship
Once Only
by jonivan
You and Me Against the World
Paul Williams
Reach Out for Your Dreams
I Promise You My Love
Thank You for Being My Parents
A Mother's Love
A Friend Forever
gentle freedom, gentle courage
diane westlake
You Are Always My Friend
When We Are Apart
It's Nice to Know Someone Like You
by Peter McWilliams
These Words Are for You
by Leonard Nimoy
It Isn't Always Easy
My Sister, My Friend
Thoughts of Love
Thoughts of You, My Friend
You Mean So Much To Me
Don't Ever Give Up Your Dreams

Love
Isn't Always
Easy

A collection of poems on love and
making it work... because it's worth it

Edited by Susan Polis Schutz

Blue Mountain Press ™.

Boulder, Colorado

Library of Congress Number: 82-74104
ISBN: 0-88396-182-2

Manufactured in the United States of America
First Printing: January, 1983

The following works have previously appeared in Blue Mountain Arts publications:

"Why do I put you," by Susan Polis Schutz. Copyright © Continental Publications, 1979. "In order to have," by Susan Polis Schutz. Copyright © Stephen Schutz and Susan Polis Schutz, 1980. "Love is" and "I dislike so much," by Susan Polis Schutz. Copyright © Stephen Schutz and Susan Polis Schutz, 1982. "Since I spend so much time with you," by Susan Polis Schutz. Copyright © Stephen Schutz and Susan Polis Schutz, 1983. "I don't always know," by Jamie Delere; "I know it hasn't been easy," by Laine Parsons; and "I'm still learning about love," by Andrew Tawney. Copyright © Blue Mountain Arts, Inc., 1982. "I know it's hard for us," "I know you're going to make it," and "In the beginning," by amanda pierce; "I know things" and "We'll be okay, won't we," by Jamie Delere; "It's funny sometimes," "I Want Us to Be" and "Please understand," by Laine Parsons; and "There is a funny old saying," by Michael Rille. Copyright © Blue Mountain Arts, Inc., 1983. All rights reserved.

Thanks to the Blue Mountain Arts creative staff.

Acknowledgments appear on page 92.

Blue Mountain Press INC.

P.O. Box 4549, Boulder, Colorado 80306

CONTENTS

I know it's hard for us
    sometimes . . .
Outside forces create pressures
    that affect our lives in
        unpredictable ways
Sometimes, we let our moods
    get the better of us;
our accomplishments fall short
    of our goals;
plans fall by the wayside;
and dreams seem too distant
    to hope for anymore . . .

But deep inside, I always
    carry our love,
and I know that we must never
stop working toward making
    things better . . .
After all . . .
we chose to be in this life
        together,
and with a little effort
    and understanding
and a lot of patience and love
that's exactly the way
    we're going to stay . . .
        happily together
                forever.

— amanda pierce

In everyone's life
   there are problems to solve.
Even in the strongest relationship,
   there are differences to overcome.
It is easy to give up when confronted
   with difficulties;
to fool yourself into believing that
   perfection can be found
      somewhere else.
But true happiness and a lasting
   relationship are found
when you look inside yourself for
   solutions to the problems.

Instead of walking away when things
   get tough and blaming the other
      person,
look for compromise and forgiveness.
Caring is not a matter of convenience.
It is a commitment of one soul
   to another.
And if each gives generously of
   themselves, then both lives
      are enriched.
The problems will come and go,
   just like the changing seasons.
But unselfish love is constant
   and everlasting.

— Susan Staszewski

I don't always know
how to tell you . . .
I'm not sure
how to let you know
when I'm worried
    or wondering . . .
About whether our
    relationship
    is okay, and whether
you're as happy
as you want to be.
I want you to know . . .
that I don't always
have things figured out;
that I need your help sometimes
    and your reassurance . . .
and sometimes I need
just to have you hold me
to let me know
that it's okay
and that we'll make it
    together through the hard times,
    appreciating all the good times,
hand in hand,
love
    in
        love.

— Jamie Delere

Learning isn't easy . . .
frustration tends to set in
    quickly.
You hurt.
You feel defeated.
You want to give up—
    to quit.
You want to walk away
    and pretend it doesn't
        matter.
But you won't,
because you're not a loser—
    you're a fighter . . .

We all have to lose sometimes
    before we can win,
we have to cry sometimes
    before we can smile.
We have to hurt
    before we can be strong.
But if you keep on working
        and believing,
you'll have victory
    in the end.

— Ann Davies

I know things
  aren't always sunshine and roses
    between us . . .
but don't worry;
everybody has their ups and downs,
    their happys and sads.
It's dealing with the
clouds and the thorns,
right along with the
    flowers and smiles
that serves to strengthen our
understanding of each other.
Let's just make sure
that we always build bridges
instead of walls,
with words instead of silence,
and with trust and care and love.

— Jamie Delere

I dislike so much
the times when
I am angry at you
or when you are
angry at me
We need to
talk about our feelings more
and not harbor resentment
We need to
immediately tell each other
why we feel hurt or mad
so we can make amends
Our days are too short
to waste any time on
not being completely happy
with each other

— Susan Polis Schutz

I cannot give up my self for you
   nor do I want yours.
I cannot change my life's goals for you
   nor do I want you to change yours.
What I can do for you, for us, for a
   relationship consisting of you and me
Is to be a friend, companion, lover
A sharer of space and time
A comfort, support, giver.
Yet I can only do this if you do the same,
   As a relationship is built of
   the givings of two.
To be settled and strong in this way,
   gives peace of mind and soul . . .

So energies can be spent on our
   purposes and not the constant
   struggle of surrendering into love.

Of your own free choice you, too,
   must enter this bond—or else there
   is no bond.
It's all the energies of the universe
   that we are confronting by calling
   on love.
It takes deep understanding and
   a strength so powerful.
   A commitment of love, purpose, goals
   that can be united and separate—
   overlapping.
   There cannot be anything less
   for us.

— Joni Frankel

It's hard to be in love sometimes
with all your feelings so vulnerable
When you give your love,
there are no secure defenses
But to offer yourself is the
        ultimate gift . . .
And love can be so grand
like the feeling you get when
        the sun shines through your window
and you're warm and secure . . .
There is no substitute for having
        a special person with whom
you can share your love, your life
Love can be hard sometimes . . .
        but it's worth it.

— Johnnie Rosenauer

When two people entrust one another
with their innermost feelings,
their hearts, their lives,
the bond between them strengthens
and surrounds them until each becomes
a part of the other.
This closeness cannot be measured
by time, words or circumstance.
It is a wholeness of the soul, a silence,
and the highest form of intimacy.

—Dorie Runyon

A thought for the two of you . . .

I know you're going
    to make it . . .
It may take time
    and hard work
You may become frustrated
and at times you'll feel
    like giving up
Sometimes you may even
    wonder if it's really
            worth it
But I have confidence
    in you,
and I know you'll make it,
        if you try.

— amanda pierce

Let it never be the case
that we grow
too weary, impatient
        or fearful
to sit and talk
to one another
about our love.
Let us always remember
that just sitting
and talking
to one another
is how we discovered
our love
in the first place.

— Kele Daniels

I've spent a good part
   of my life
running away from things . . .
Escaping any type of deep
   relationship,
walking away from my beliefs . . .
But now, I've begun working
   on my self-spirituality—
I'm looking better and feeling
   better than ever before
and I know that someday soon,
everything will come together . . .

Once I am able to love myself
   for the person that I am . . .
I will know how to love someone
   as beautiful as you.

— Gail Nishimoto

Be patient with me.
Understand that I'm just beginning to
    realize
what my needs are,
and that you fill them all . . .

Be patient with me . . .
know that my mind is sometimes clouded
with not-so-distant memories
that invade my existence.

Be patient with me.
Feel the warmth that flows between us
in the hours when my head is clear
of painful thoughts of days left behind.

Be patient with me.
Reach out and accept the tenderness
I so long to give you,
although you deserve so much more.

Be patient with me.
Our time will come.

— Noreen S. Jenney

I love you.

I may not always show it
so you may not always feel it.

The problems come, not from you
but from the insecurities
I bring
to our relationship.

You are loving,
but sometimes
I am too scared,
too fearful,
too threatened
to accept love.

I will keep in mind
that you have
insecurities too,
and I will remember
you love me
even at those times
when I find it difficult
to accept love.

— Alice Cooper Richardson

If we really care . . .
care enough to work at
        our feelings—
to love not only with
        our heads,
but with our hearts—
we can make it together
        through any problems
for the rest of our
        lives.

— Kathy M. Ward

It is hectic times like these,
when we find ourselves too
    concerned
with the affairs of the world,
that make the private moments
we have reserved for the
    two of us
so much more special than
any others in life—
For it is those times
    of serene togetherness
that we can really feel
how deep our love is for
    one another,
and we can truly appreciate
that there is nothing more precious
    in all of life
than our love
    for each other.

— Daniel Haughian

There is no easy way,
but there's a way.
We both could use some
          understanding,
trust would help;
The journey of a
          thousand miles
begins with just one step.
And is love not worth
          the price
we'll have to pay?
There is no easy way,
but there's a way.

— Willie Nelson

It is only through magic
   that we have come this far . . .
   through the barriers
   that the world saw fit
   to place in our way.
From deep within, we found the courage
   and the strength to carry on,
   moving forward, through the tears . . .
   to reach, touch, and recreate
   the truth, and hope, and faith
   that is our love.
Together . . .
   we are stronger than either of us alone . . .
   hand in hand, we will face
   tomorrow and the world.

— Kathy Pepin

To begin a new life together
does not mean that we must forget
the lives that each of us
    leaves behind;
but rather
we should remember the differences
that brought us here;
and keep alive the memories of what
you and I are
in our pursuit of what we can
become together.

— laura west

A true relationship
knows of but one great thing:
  to give of one's self
boundlessly
in order to find one's self
  richer,
    deeper,
      better.

— Emma Goldman

It's funny sometimes how
—even though we love
and trust one another—
we still can leave so many words
unsaid between us,
so many wishes unspoken.
There are times, I'm sure,
when we've both wanted to be
listened to, to be held—
but our inner words and
    our outer signals
were too quiet to be
noticed by the other . . .

If we were able to be
as close and as communicative
as I would like us to be,
hardly a word would go unspoken
    that needed to be heard;
hardly a touch would go unheeded
    that needed to be felt;
hardly a day would go by
    without us
        falling more in love.

— Laine Parsons

There is a funny old saying, one that says,
"If you don't ride a bicycle,
you don't fall off!"
What it means to say, of course, is
if you do put a lot of energy into something,
you are bound to make mistakes;
and if you take a lot of risks,
you are bound to tumble here and there.
But remember this: that if you persist,
you will arrive at the destination of your choice.
And if you do occasionally fall in the process,
you'll learn much more than if you don't.

So try, and do, and discover all that you can be.

And take me with you . . .
    in spirit, as you go,
so you'll know that
I'll always be beside you
wishing for nothing but the best.

— Michael Rille

In order to have
a successful relationship
you need to put out of your mind
any lessons learned
from previous relationships
because if you carry
a sensitivity or fear with you
you won't be acting freely
and you won't let yourself
be really known

In order to have
a successful relationship
it is essential that both people
be completely open and honest

— Susan Polis Schutz

I love you . . .
   I really do.
I'm a little afraid,
      but I know that
only when we learn to trust,
   and to risk rejection
will we really come to know
      the warmth of each other
and find peace in discovering
      the beautiful hidden parts
         inside.

— Sue Mitchell

Love is the
greatest of all feelings . . .

a feeling
that works wonders.

— Anton Makarenko

There is no difficulty that enough love
will not conquer; No disease that enough
love will not heal; No door that enough love
will not open; No gulf that enough love will
not bridge; No wall that enough love will not
throw down; No sin that enough love
will not redeem . . .

It makes no difference how deeply
seated may be the trouble;
How hopeless the outlook; How muddled
the tangle; How great the mistake.
A sufficient realization of love will dissolve
it all . . . If only you could love enough you
would be the happiest and most powerful
being in the world . . .

— Emmet Fox

Love is
   being happy for the other person
      when they are happy
   being sad for the person
      when they are sad
   being together in good times
   and being together in bad times
Love is the source of strength

Love is
   being honest with yourself at all times
   being honest with the other person at all times
   telling, listening, respecting the truth,
   and never pretending
Love is the source of reality

Love is
   an understanding so complete that
   you feel as if you are a part of the other person
   accepting the other person just the way they are
   and not trying to change them to be something else
Love is the source of unity

Love is
   the freedom to pursue your own desires
   while sharing your experiences with the other person
   the growth of one individual alongside of
   and together with the growth of another individual
Love is the source of success. . .

Love is
   the excitement of planning things together
   the excitement of doing things together
Love is the source of the future

Love is
   the fury of the storm
   the calm in the rainbow
Love is the source of passion

Love is
   giving and taking in a daily situation
   being patient with each other's needs and desires
Love is the source of sharing

Love is
   knowing that the other person
   will always be with you regardless of what happens
   missing the other person when they are away
   but remaining near in heart at all times
Love is the source of security

Love is
   the
source
   of
life

— Susan Polis Schutz

I realize that our love has not always
   been so contented . . .
We've had our share of rough times
   and rugged hills we've struggled
      and managed to climb.
We have cried as well as laughed,
   failed as well as succeeded,
and refused to let go of
   each other's grasp . . .
but even if I had the power,
   there is not a solitary thing
      that I would rearrange . . .
Ours is a love
   fashioned by God
      out of pure love
         for you and me.

— Betty Mire

The bond that holds two people together is not always a strand of silk, but a length of rope, rough and coarse . . . Whatever the bond, it is neither stronger nor weaker than the two people who would have it so . . . As long as they choose to travel the same road, neither their fortunes nor their misfortunes can be divided . . . If one laughs, they both laugh; if one cries, they both cry; if one lives, they both live; and indeed, if one dies, they both die. . . . If one separates his or her needs as more important than the other's, then they are not together . . . and while one should not stand in the shadow of the other, neither should seek the sun without the other . . . for the bond to work, both must be together in all things.

— Tim Martin

I must admit,
when I met you
I was afraid.
Afraid of love,
for I had
failed before.
Afraid of goodbyes,
for I had
to say them
too many times...

Now . . . I'm no longer
scared of love,
for what I have
with you
is so beautiful.
As for goodbyes . . .

I still get scared
when I think
of the word;
so let's make
a promise . . .
that we'll never
use that word;
and that we'll
just try to
love each other
as much
as we possibly can.

— Kitty Closson

I tried to get angry at you for my blues today.
I sat down and began to list all of your faults
   all of the reasons why I should forget you
   all of the excuses for my hurting you.
But each time I wrote one fault,
   I remembered a dozen reasons why I cared.
And after adding up all the points about you,
   I found the bad wasn't really so bad,
   and the good was really good.
I could never be angry with you.

— Michael J. Mulvena

Since I spend so much time with you
thinking about you
talking to you
doing things with you
I must accept any faults
   that you might have
and you must accept any faults
   that I might have
and we must not let these bother us
   but rather
we must ignore them
I cannot expect you to be perfect
you cannot expect me to be perfect
No one is . . .

We must concentrate on
   all that is good in each other
so that our relationship
   will remain positive and
happy
forever

— Susan Polis Schutz

How can I help you?
   Please just ask
      or give some sign . . .
      and I will be there
I will never knowingly
   let you down,
but if I do, please forgive me
and know that
   I could never hurt you.

I want to walk with you
   through any difficulty you have,
and if you need to be alone,
   I will understand.
But please let me know . . .
   if I can help.

— Sue Mitchell

To love
means to communicate
to the other
that you are all for him,
that you will never fail him
or let him down
when he needs you,
but that you
will always
be standing by.

— Ashley Montagu

I Want Us to Be . . .

I know that
things are sort of difficult
right now for us . . .
but nobody ever said
it was going to be easy;
especially something
as important as the
blending of two lives into one.

I know that it's hard sometimes.
There are so many things
to be concerned about . . .

But at least we can do our part
by trying to realize what
the problems are, and then by
being flexible enough
to deal with them.

And if we work at it,
if we really try . . .
we can become like a willow tree;
one that bends in the wind
instead of breaking,
and one that just grows stronger
and becomes more beautiful
with the passing of time.

— Laine Parsons

Our life together will be worth
waiting for . . .
Time is our only obstacle and
like all things, it too will pass;
perhaps slowly, but nonetheless,
the day will come when finally
we will have the beautiful life
　　we've planned on.
　　And then we'll say
　　that it was surely worth
　　the wait.

— Susan Santacroce

The present time is most
    important
I don't really care about
    the past
Having you as a part of my life now
    is what counts
Having your trust and understanding
    is important.

— piera mirabile

A relationship
has to be more
than words.

It has to be sharing
pleasure in new ideas.
It has to be drawing on differences
to become closer.

It has to be caring
when the other person is hurting.
It has to be touching
when words aren't enough.

It has to be accepting
that the other person needs time alone.
It has to be building a solid foundation
towards future love and happiness.

But most important,
a relationship
needs trust in each other.

— Carol Mann

The Keys to Love

The key to love is understanding . . .
　　the ability to comprehend
　　not only the spoken word,
　　but those unspoken gestures,
　　the little things that say
　　so much by themselves.

The key to love is forgiveness . . .
　　to accept each other's faults
　　and pardon mistakes,
　　without forgetting—
　　but with remembering
　　what you learn from them .

The key to love is trust . . .
　　though dark doubts
　　lay in hollowed thoughts,
　　it must shine brightly on
　　with reassuring radiance
　　that suppresses fear with faith.

The key to love is sharing . . .
　　facing your good fortunes
　　as well as the bad, together;
　　both conquering problems—
　　forever searching for ways
　　to intensify your happiness. . .

The key to love is giving . . .
    without thought of return,
    but with the hope of just
    a simple smile
    and by giving-in, but never up.

The key to love is respect . . .
    realizing that you are
    two separate people
    with different ideas;
    that you don't belong to each other,
    but that you belong with each other
    and share a mutual bond.

The key to love is inside us all . . .
    it takes time and patience
    to unlock all the ingredients
    that will take you to its threshold;
    it is a continual learning process
    that demands a lot of work . . .
    but the rewards are more than
    worth the effort . . .
And you
    are the key
        to me.

— Robert M. Millay

I promise . . .

I will not blame you for my bad feelings,
nor ask you to make me feel good.

I will share my real self with you and
take responsibility for my own feelings.

I will treat all our intimacies with absolute
confidence and gratitude for your trust.

I will take your desires and needs seriously
and never disregard or ignore them.

I will hold myself accountable to allowing
you to fulfill and express your own life.

I will risk new ways for us to grow in
closeness, trust and mutual respect . . .

I will love whatsoever I find in you,
and cherish every moment we have
together.

— Jene Miller

Love—can carry us to the moon and beyond, to the farthest star that breathes everlasting light, but we must be willing to win love. We must pay with patience, with faith, and understanding, and much, much more. The price is high, but the earth holds no greater treasure.

— Rowland R. Hoskins, Jr.

If ever I did,
I never intended to clip your wings
for one who doesn't have the freedom
    to fly
will surely find a way to get free.

If ever I did,
I never intended to be jealous,
but I am just a person who is still
    a lot like a little child,
and sometimes I'm terribly unsure
    of myself. . .

If ever I did,
I never intended to change you,
for if you were to change,
you wouldn't be the person
    that I fell in love with,
and our love might fade.

If ever I did,
I never intended to make you dependent
for dependence stunts personal growth,
    not just for one,
        but for both people.

If never I did,
I always intended to simply share
    my love with you
  for your love is my life,
and my life is nothing
    without you.

— Thomas R. Dudley

Sometimes it's hard for me
to make a commitment—
even though I know I love you and
I want you by my side.
Sometimes it seems that
the more I need you,
the more I push you away.
But if you could just see beyond the
obstacles I often put there,
you would see that . . .
I really do want you,
I really do need you,
I really do love you.

— Doris Amundson Arnold

Many times I think about all we've come through in our time, and I almost can't believe how good my life has been . . . because of you.

I think back to easier days that we wished would go on forever. Then, I think of how much we've grown because they couldn't and I'm glad.

I think about the hurts we have known and how we wished we didn't have to suffer. But now I know that our suffering came in the form of pain, but left us rich with blessings.

I am wealthier than anyone I know . . . because of our friendship. And our suffering from time to time is a small price to pay for the journey we travel in our love.

— Diana Marie-Chavez

Why do I put you
through such misery
when I love you
so much
Why do I act so moody
with you
when I love you
so much
I must be going through something
which needs a lot of introspection—
the only way I'll get over it is
to understand it
and not take it out
on anyone else
especially
you
whom I love
so much

— Susan Polis Schutz

We have got to communicate—
We can't let the minutes,
   hours, days
   go by any longer
without understanding the hurt.
I've got to know why things are
   the way they are.
We have got to communicate . . .

— Rick Norman

A good relationship means
listening to each other, and
   really hearing—not only
the spoken words, but also
the hopes, fears and insecurities
behind the words.
   I think we hear each other.

— Linda Darkes Kounitz

I know it hasn't been easy
for you lately,
and I can't even begin to tell you
how much you've been on my mind.
It isn't easy for me . . .
feeling so far away from you
when I want to be close enough
to hold you
and look at you
and to tell you
   with all my heart
that everything's going
to be alright.

— Laine Parsons

Look back and see the goodness,
the happiness you've shared.
Remember the fun times,
   first experiences
and the beauty of a sunrise.
Look back to treasured memories;
forget the sorrows and the hurts.
Simply recall all of the
   loveliness that
you've cherished for so long.

And once you've looked back,
then look forward . . .
to the very best part of your
      life—
the part which is still to come.

— Gayle Rosenfeld

the moments spent sharing
    with you
are the best part of my life.
our relationship is so fragile;
    so new.
let us find the courage
to give of ourselves
    to each other.
the risk of caring
    is so small.
        the reward,
            so great.

— Vicki S. Mossman

I hope that you can be
   whatever you need to be with me.
I hope that you sense
   enough love from me
to feel easy about smiling
   when you need to smile,
     and crying when you need to cry.
I really hope that
   you feel secure enough with me
     to be silent
       or to show your needs
         or just to ask for a hug.
Feeling that secure is important . . .
     I know;
because I need that feeling
     of security . . . from you, too.

— Sue Mitchell

Everyone has their mountain to climb
    and their ocean to sail.
Let's climb and sail ours together . . .
hand in hand, heart in heart.

— Mary N. Shader

I will not . . .

I will not judge you . . .
I will not bring up the past . . .
   for fear of wiping out
   the present.
I will not possess you . . .
   even though I want to
   own your every breath.
I will not plan our every moment . . .
   surprises are more fun.
I will not lie to you . . .
   even when the truth
   will hurt you more.
I will not try to change you . . .
   I accept you "as is."
I will not take away your pain . . .
   you need it to grow on, too.
I will not have expectations of you . . .
   the ones you have of yourself
   are great enough.
I will not stop loving you . . .
   no matter what.

— Kathleen O'Brien

Is it okay to feel afraid?
Because I am . . . sometimes
    afraid of taking a chance,
    afraid of losing,
    even afraid of winning sometimes.
I'm scared to love too much,
    scared to hold on too tight
    when you may want to be free;
    scared of letting go
    when I need you to hold me.
        And I need to know
            if it's okay to feel afraid,
        because sometimes I am . . .
        because I love you so much.

— Daumont Valentine

Let's just be together
and enjoy our relationship
for what it is right now,
and not worry about
where it is going
or how it will be
in the future.
Let's be honest and open
with our feelings and emotions,
just be ourselves—together
and bring out the very best
in each other . . .
Let's just be together.

— Debra Kay Sticht

Coming
together
is a beginning;

Keeping
together
is progress;

Working
together
is success.

— Anonymous

Sometimes the pressures of life,
   the worries and frustrations
build walls between us.
You see things your way
   and I see things my way . . .
and for a short time
we forget what we really mean
         to each other.

Through patience and understanding
   the harmony is restored,
and we can share life's beauty
         together again.

— Susan Staszewski

I'm still learning about love,
so please be patient with me
when things go wrong, or
    when I hurt your feelings.
We have so much to look forward to,
and the time goes by so quickly . . .
that we should promise
never to allow a misunderstanding
to continue beyond a brief time.

We will deal with our concerns
as they come up . . . and our love
    will just get better, because . . .
we learn by doing,
and we grow by experiencing . . .

We've learned enough already to know
that love is made up of all things,
 the good with the difficult times,
 the quiet with the talkative times,
 the questions with the answers.

And even when I don't seem to know
 anything else . . .
I know that you're the answer
and the best thing in my life.

— Andrew Tawney

In the beginning
I was a little frightened
   by our closeness
I had never before had
   someone in my life
who cared so much or felt
   so deeply
or who means as much to me
   as you. . .

I was scared of what might
    happen if ever you had to go
I was afraid of being hurt
or even worse, of somehow
    hurting you
But now, I feel more secure
    in our relationship
and I don't worry so much
    about the future . . .
because there are so many
    good things to think about
like you and me
and all the wonderful things
    we're going to do
        together.

— amanda pierce

We'll be okay, won't we?

The one thing that matters
more to me than anything else
   in the world . . . is you and me.
You are my world.
You're the one who gets all
   my love and my wishes and my prayers.
But somehow . . . despite all my
   best intentions,
I never feel quite safe enough
   or sure enough
to rest assured that I'll always be
able to make you happy. . .

I need to know.
I need you more than my words can say.
I need to always feel
   the warm peaceful feeling
   that I get when you hold me.
I need to experience the beauty
   of our love that I gently receive
   when we caress.

I need for us to remember
   all the love that's been given
   and all the love that will unfold
   each day, between the wonder of you
      and the warmth of me.

And sometimes,
   I just need to know
     that we'll be okay . . . won't we?

— Jamie Delere

Please understand
that I've got to go slow;
that I need a little time . . .
you see, I'm still trying
   to get to the point
where I'm happy with myself;
   where I'm confident
      and safe and secure
         just being me.

I know that it might
take a little while,
and a bit of patience,
but when I do get there—
when I reach the point
where I want to be—
I hope and pray that
I'll be able to open the door
and on the other side,
   see you, smiling so warmly,
      looking back at me.

— Laine Parsons

ACKNOWLEDGMENTS

We gratefully acknowledge the permission granted by the following authors, publishers and authors' representatives to reprint poems and excerpts from their publications.

Susan Staszewski for "In everyone's life" and "Sometimes the pressures of life," by Susan Staszewski. Copyright © Susan Staszewski, 1982. All rights reserved. Reprinted by permission.

Ann Davies for "Learning isn't easy . . . ," by Ann Davies. Copyright © Ann Davies, 1983. All rights reserved. Reprinted by permission.

Joni Frankel for "I cannot give up my self," by Joni Frankel. Copyright © Joni Frankel, 1982. All rights reserved. Reprinted by permission.

Johnnie Rosenauer for "It's hard to be in love sometimes," by Johnnie Rosenauer. Copyright © Johnnie Rosenauer, 1983. All rights reserved. Reprinted by permission.

Dorie Runyon for "When two people entrust one another," by Dorie Runyon. Copyright © Dorie Runyon, 1983. All rights reserved. Reprinted by permission.

Kele Daniels for "Let it never be the case," by Kele Daniels. Copyright © Kele Daniels, 1982. All rights reserved. Reprinted by permission.

Gail Nishimoto for "I've spent a good part of my life," by Gail Nishimoto. Copyright © Gail Nishimoto, 1983. All rights reserved. Reprinted by permission.

Noreen S. Jenney for "Be patient with me," by Noreen S. Jenney. Copyright © Noreen S. Jenney, 1983. All rights reserved. Reprinted by permission.

Alice Cooper Richardson for "I love you," by Alice Cooper Richardson. Copyright © Alice Cooper Richardson, 1982. All rights reserved. Reprinted by permission.

Kathy M. Ward for "If we really care . . . ," by Kathy M. Ward. Copyright © Kathy M. Ward, 1983. All rights reserved. Reprinted by permission.

Daniel Haughian for "It is hectic times like these," by Daniel Haughian. Copyright © Daniel Haughian, 1983. All rights reserved. Reprinted by permission.

Tree International for "There is no easy way," by Willie Nelson. Copyright © 1961 Tree Publishing Co., Inc. All rights reserved. Reprinted by permission.

Kathy Pepin for "It is only through magic," by Kathy Pepin. Copyright © Kathy Pepin, 1983. All rights reserved. Reprinted by permission.

Laura West for "To begin a new life together," by Laura West. Copyright © Laura West, 1982. All rights reserved. Reprinted by permission.

Sue Mitchell for "I love you . . . ," "How can I help you," and "I hope that you can be," by Sue Mitchell. Copyright © Sue Mitchell, 1983. All rights reserved. Reprinted by permission.

Betty Mire for "I realize that our love," by Betty Mire. Copyright © Betty Mire, 1983. All rights reserved. Reprinted by permission.

Tim Martin for "The bond that holds two people," by Tim Martin. Copyright © Tim Martin, 1983. All rights reserved. Reprinted by permission.

Kitty Closson for "I must admit," by Kitty Closson. Copyright © Kitty Closson, 1983. All rights reserved. Reprinted by permission.

Michael J. Mulvena for "I tried to get angry at you," by Michael J. Mulvena. Copyright © Michael J. Mulvena, 1983. All rights reserved. Reprinted by permission.